REAL ESTATE WEALTH

Remove the Guesswork from Investing and Create a Six-Figure Strategy

Kito J. Johnson

Copyright and Disclaimer

Copyright © 2018 All rights reserved.
Written by Kito J. Johnson
www.kitojjohnson.com

This book nor any portion thereof may be reproduced, stored in a retrieval system or transmitted in any form by any means, electronic, mechanical, photocopying, recording, or otherwise without prior permission from the author except for the use of brief quotations where the author is given credit.

Limit of Liability: The information contained within this book is strictly for education purposes. If you wish to apply ideas contained herein, you are taking full responsibility for your actions. The author has made every effort to ensure that the accuracy of the information within this book was correct at the time of publication. The author does not assume or hereby claim any liability to any party for any loss, damage, or disruption caused by errors and omissions, whether such errors or omissions resulted from accident, negligence, or any other cause.

Any trademarks, service marks, product names and named features are assumed to be property of their respective owners and are used only for reference. No endorsement is implied from the use of any of these terms. Finally, be wise. Nothing in this book is intended to replace common sense or legal, accounting, or professional advice. This content is only meant to inform.

Published by Melchizedek Global Publishing
Roswell, Georgia
www.melchizedekglobal.net

Cover and Interior Graphic Design: Joel Sousa
Interior Layout: Sandeep Likhar

Print ISBN: 978-0-9989502-3-5
EBook ISBN: 978-0-9989502-4-2
Published in the United States of America

Dedication

This book is dedicated to my children, Immanuel and Imani. You are powerful beyond measure! Thank you for fueling my passion and supporting my call to empower the masses.

Acknowledgements

Mom, thank you for teaching me the importance of having a strong and powerful work ethic. Dad, thanks for imparting such a deep entrepreneurial drive in me. I *am* because you both *are*!

Thank you to the coaches in my life who encouraged this project – Lisa Nichols, Tajuana Ross, Lamar and Ronnie Tyler, and Dr. Connie Williams.

Table of Contents

Dedication 3

Acknowledgements 4

Table of Contents 5

Foreword 7

Introduction 11

Chapter 1 - Finding Your *Why* 19

Chapter 2 - The Big Three Questions for New Investors ... 35

Chapter 3 - Active or Passive Investing? 51

Chapter 4 - The Big Three Investing Strategies 55

Chapter 5 - Tax Benefits for Real Estate Investors 73

Chapter 6 - Finding Property 79

Chapter 7 - Connecting With Sellers 87

Chapter 8 - Networking 93

Chapter 9 - Avoiding Pitfalls 97

Chapter 10 - Your Next Steps 103

Chapter 11 - Dream Turned Reality 105

Glossary 109

Your Six-Figure Strategy 115

About the Author 121

Foreword

"Wow!"

That's what I thought the first time I sat on the other end of a phone call with Kito J. Johnson. This guy was the real deal when it came to real estate, and this was particularly impressive in an industry where there are so many self-proclaimed experts who don't *really* have any actual expertise.

He knew about wholesaling, flipping, buying-to-hold and everything in between. Utilizing his limited free time, he had created a successful real estate business and was teaching others how they could get started on their own.

For the next hour we talked about how my company, which helps businesses leverage online opportunities, could help get his message to the masses online. I was game because I knew the world needed to know the ideas he was sharing.

These ideas are important because there is an opportunity that lies before both you and me. This is an opportunity to go beyond what we've known into a realm that many of us may be unfamiliar with. The opportunity I am referencing is *legacy*.

Webster's dictionary defines legacy as *"a gift by will especially of money or other personal property."*

While a *legacy* should be the norm, many of us are not familiar with it because we were never handed this type of gift.

This is a realm that many of us were not necessarily born into, but even so, we have a chance to shift the future right now. We have the ability to leave a legacy into which our children and our children's children will be born, a legacy of wealth that enables them to bypass the issues that come from lack.

When we talk about wealth, there are often misconceptions that, in order to have it, we must give up our faith, our principles, or even who we are. But what you'll learn from Kito's words in the pages of this book is that you can have wealth abundantly without compromising your convictions.

Before you tap into wealth you have to realize that there are things that are holding you back. When you see an opportunity in front of you and you can't step into that opportunity, oftentimes it is because of fear. That fear may be springing from self-limiting beliefs or even a lack of understanding. But within the pages of this book you will begin to transform yourself (and more importantly, your thinking) to understand that on the other side of fear is the legacy that we're talking about. On the other side of fear is the opportunity. On the other side of fear is a healthy amount of risk, and that risk is what we'll need to engage with instead of retreat from in order to create the shift we desire for those that come behind us.

So you must push through. You have to push through, and this book you're reading is the first step in the process. You'll find out shortly that Kito is not only an expert, but is also an authority on simultaneously walking in faith while walking toward wealth. His vehicle of choice for this is real estate, and he has the ability to take extremely complex principles and break them down into laymen's terms that anyone can, not only grasp, but also activate.

You will learn that God has been made more available to you than what you currently see, perhaps more than you currently even desire. The key is to combine your faith with your knowledge in order to see the results.

So again, I encourage you to grab a pen and read through the pages of this book, and then read them again until you have understanding. Then most importantly, realize that nothing happens until you take action. To read this entire book from front cover to back cover without implementing the strategies, techniques, and tips that Kito shares will do no service to you or those who are coming after you.

So after you've listened, after you've learned, after you've read, after you've highlighted, you must put this message into practice. You must figure out what the next steps are, how you can move forward, and connect with Kito and the opportunities he has available to you beyond the book in order to reach success quickly.

There is a shortcut to success. And that shortcut is getting with people who have already been where you want to go, finding people who have already blazed the path so that you don't have to create a new one, and grabbing hold of everything you need in order to reach the next level of success.

Lamar Tyler
Founder, Traffic, Sales & Profit
www.lamartyler.com

Introduction

Welcome! My name is Kito J. Johnson, founder and CEO of Buy n Sell, Inc., an Atlanta based real estate brokerage, and founder of The Generational Wealth University.

I discovered my passion for real estate when I was a teen. I remember looking forward to getting my license to drive. Starting at age 13 I started counting down the years, months, and days until my 16th birthday (much like my son has recently!). After getting my license, while others my age were enjoying driving to the movies, amusement parks, and the mall, I was more excited about driving through new construction neighborhoods and admiring the architecture, construction quality, and finish details.

Sometimes I feel as if I stumbled into real estate (just like all other major blessings in my life).

At age 20, through a family friend, I became aware of a home that had recently been vacated. The home was in disrepair and definitely needed plenty of TLC, but this did not concern me because I had grown up around my father's construction company. However, though I was armed with my father's passion for entrepreneurship, I still had no real estate experience.

The condition of the home was pretty bad, so bad in fact, that as we walked through the house, dirt would jump from the fibers of the carpet. Doors were hanging off and walls that desperately needed paint were decorated with holes. The dated kitchen was a mess, so much so that even as we stood in it to discuss our renovation plan, the floor gave way and my dad fell into the basement! Thank God it wasn't a long fall. He was fine but you get the idea that the house was not in good shape.

In spite of all of this, I knew that with a little sweat equity this would make a great home for the family I intended to start. What's most interesting to me today is how the deal came together. With no prior real estate education, I found myself in the tax assessor's office researching the homeowner. After finding that information, I dialed 411 directory assistance (the internet wasn't quite as powerful then) and received the owner's telephone number. I reached out to him and expressed my interest in acquiring his recently vacated home. I figured the chances of him being interested in selling were pretty high since he had recently come out of an undesirable landlord-tenant situation.

I called the owner and asked if he was interested in selling his vacant property. He replied, "Actually, yes! My tenants just moved out and I have my contractor over at the property doing some work right now." I indicated that I wanted to buy the home in its as-is condition. The owner instructed me to make an offer as soon as possible and, if agreeable, he would stop his contractors.

I offered $76,000 and went under contract to buy the home. I immediately reached out to a mortgage company. The lender sent an appraiser to determine the value of the home for a loan when I was informed that the home was in too much disrepair to qualify for any conventional financing. Having no knowledge of available investment loan options, I went back to the seller and asked for the ability to take possession of the home with a six-month window to renovate it and obtain long term financing once the renovation was complete. Though unaware of it at the time, I realize now that I had negotiated a lease option contract.

I was stumbling into my purpose. Learning by trial and error the strategies that I would later teach as an investor and coach.

Six months later I did as promised. The home was renovated to the point that it would qualify for traditional financing and it became my primary residence.

Still stumbling into my purpose, some months later I found myself channel surfing when I came across a guy named Robert Kiyosaki. He was sitting on the couch of a lady named Oprah. He was an invited guest to discuss his book, *Rich Dad, Poor Dad*. I purchased the book and read it from cover to cover in a few days. I suddenly realized that I had accidentally already begun to employ some of the strategies he discussed.

Still stumbling, some weeks later I found myself at a grocery store where I met a gentleman who was an investor and property manager. I told him about my experience reading the book *Rich Dad, Poor Dad*, and that I lived in a house that I had renovated. One thing led to another, and he made me an offer I couldn't refuse. He said, "Kito, if you'll allow me to sell you your next house, I'll put a tenant in your existing property and manage it for free." I thought, sounds like a deal to me.

I found a new house, moved, and made that property my first rental. I was officially a real estate investor. I stumbled into what I would later discover was my purpose for existence. At times it's hard to believe that 20 years have passed. Now, as a licensed real estate broker in several states and a coach and trainer to countless investors around the country, I've got over 1,000 transactions under my belt.

I am very excited to share my knowledge with you so you can learn the foundations of real estate investing and take control of your financial future. If you read to the end of this book, you will have a clear, actionable plan for building your own profitable real estate business. This is the same blueprint that I've used to build and support a team of investors who have completed over a quarter of a billion dollars in residential real estate transactions in multiple states around the country.

A Real Estate License Isn't Required

I am both a licensed real estate broker and also an investor, which means I bring an interesting dynamic to the marketplace. I like to describe my team as being bilingual because we speak both the language of traditional real estate as well as the language of a real estate investor. Speaking both languages came naturally to me, not just because of my passion, but also because I started as an investor before becoming a licensed real estate agent. Since this dual understanding was so natural for me, I initially took its value for granted.

It wasn't until I began hosting my Buy n Sell Atlanta networking and educational meetings that I realized the great deficit of knowledge in this area. The reality is that the average real estate agent has very little knowledge about the world of real estate investing and, of those who do, there is an even smaller percentage who understand the methods you will discover as you read this book.

Let me be clear that you do not need a real estate license to be an investor. The strategies you will learn in this book in no way require you to obtain a real estate license or degree. A real estate license is required if you are representing a buyer or seller in a transaction (for example, if you are working with a buyer to assist them in finding a home to purchase or if you are working with a seller to list their home in order to find a buyer). The distinction as an investor is that you are the buyer and/or the seller. A license is not required to buy or sell for yourself.

Often aspiring investors who are wondering if they should go to school to become a licensed real estate agent approach me. My response tends to be the same every time: if you want a portion of your career to include helping other people sell their homes or find homes to purchase, then not only *should you* get your license, but you are *required by law* to have a license. However, if you're only pursuing real estate as a means to build real estate wealth personally, then I do not recommend getting a real estate license.

Some of the things you will learn in this book are:

How to analyze the "Big Three" investing strategies to determine which approach best fits your situation.

The three questions you MUST ask yourself before beginning (or continuing) your investing career.

How to find the time, money and resources to create success in your business (even if you think it's not possible).

Many other insights from my 20-plus-year career as a real estate investor, broker, and coach.

I wrote this book as a blueprint for people in our communities to create a more prosperous future. Of the many ways to create wealth for yourself and your family, I believe real estate provides the greatest opportunity to create a legacy that will impact your children and your children's children for generations to come.

Personally, my *Why* has everything to do with my two children. I'm determined to build generational wealth that ensures their future will be prosperous AND that teaches them the tools they need to build on the success I'm creating. Psalm 127:3 speaks to this. It says: *"Children are a heritage from the Lord".*

In addition to wealth or business, legacy can exist in many forms. For example, legacy is also built by instilling in the next generation the core principles by which you've lived your life. Whether its faith, wisdom, mindset, or morals, instilling the very best of these into your family doesn't cost a dime, but it will leave a remarkable impact.

I believe that more important than what I leave *for* my children is what I leave *IN* them.

How to Get the Most Out of This Book:

1. **Read it in full AT LEAST two times.** This will help you thoroughly grasp some of the more advanced concepts.
2. **Complete the exercises.** Throughout the book I will ask you to answer questions and analyze your current situation. Have a notebook handy to

specifically document your thoughts and revelations as you go through the materials.
3. **Use the Glossary section in the back of the book** if you don't know what certain real estate terms mean.
4. **Believe in yourself.** The greatest things in life happen by learning backwards and looking forward. So forget anything from your past that's holding you back, grab hold of the lessons, and understand that you are now starting a new chapter.
5. **Reach out to me for help.** I've personally helped many new and veteran investors grow their real estate businesses. My team and I would love to be of service to you as you embark on this journey!

To your investing success!

Kito j Johnson

Founder, Generational Wealth University
www.kitojjohnson.com

1 Finding Your *Why*

After spending over 20 years in the real estate business, I can tell you that the most successful investors are driven by a deep *Why*. That *Why* motivates them every day. It keeps them focused and persistent through good times and bad. It also keeps their bigger vision at the front of their mind at all times.

My goal in this initial chapter is to help you crystalize your *Why* so that you are internally motivated to create success and prosperity for yourself and your family. With this goal in mind, we're going to look at five topics: Wealth, Mindset, Abundance, Goals, and Expectations. Make sure to spend time thinking through the questions in the chapter and writing down your thoughts in your journal and in the spaces provided.

Let's begin!

Wealth

What do YOU believe about wealth?

Figure 1.1

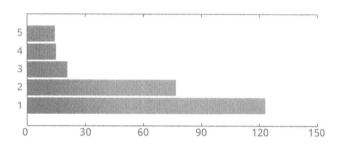

Henry Ford once said, "Whether you think you can or think you can't, you're right." So let's dive deeper to consider this important question.

Over the last two centuries, about 90% of the world's millionaires have been created by investing in real estate. While that's a staggering statistic, here is one that is even more interesting: 100% of the 10% of millionaires who did *not* earn their wealth from real estate investing realize that real estate is the best vehicle to *maintain* the wealth that they have built.

Keep this statistic in mind, because when you approach wealth building like the most successful people in the world, you give yourself the best chance to build generational wealth for your family.

See Figure 1.1.

While most people think of wealth as having a lot of money or possessions, I want to suggest a different definition that goes beyond material things. **I believe that "being wealthy" also means that you're able to make decisions without being restricted by finances.**

For example, "being wealthy" means you can send your child to a preferred school at your complete discretion without restrictions. In other words, wealth is freedom. Wealth is having options.

Take a moment to write down your thoughts about what you believe about wealth:

_____

_____

_____

_____

_____

_____

Mindset

What do you believe about yourself, your skills, your talents, and your destiny?

If you want to create success in real estate, you must understand that YOU are your greatest asset. No matter how many mistakes you've made in the past, you still hold the key to success for yourself. You can only use this power if you believe you have it!

Think about it like this...

Your beliefs create your thoughts.

Your thoughts create your actions.

Your actions create your results.

Your results create your life.

So choose your thoughts and beliefs carefully, because they show up everywhere in your life.

I got my entrepreneurial spirit from my dad. When I was a kid, he owned a successful construction business, so I learned from him how to have a business mindset. However, I also witnessed his business partner run off with $140,000 of his money. This was a very hard time for our whole family, but my dad picked himself up and crawled out of the hole that had been created for him. As hard as it was, he knew he needed to look forward, not backwards.

This tough experience taught me that pursuing big dreams goes hand-in-hand with risk. I saw that all of my dad's challenges in business actually made him a better entrepreneur.

Perhaps you know someone who has failed in real estate investing. Maybe *you* have tried your hand at real estate investing (or some other type of entrepreneurship endeavor) in the past, and it didn't work out well. Remember this:

Past results do NOT dictate future results.

Just because you failed once does not mean that you are a failure for life. As long as you're committed to learning from your mistakes, all the challenges you face will be used to create the foundation of your success.

There is one more important point to understand about mindset, and that is *trust your gut!* When I acquired my first investment property, I was simply acting in the moment and trusting my gut.

I was only 20 years old when that opportunity fell into my lap. I didn't know much about house flipping, but I decided to follow through with purchasing, fixing, and ultimately selling the property for profit. I just figured out the logistics along the way.

I acted solely on faith, without hesitation, and I believe that God honors faith. Some people talk about doing something for years and years but never decide to act on it. I believe God appreciates the decisions we make – even those that don't pan out to be the best – over the failure to make any decisions at all. **The fact that you made a decision, whether right or wrong, was in and of itself an act of faith.**

Think about it! Your willingness to act on something can literally change your whole life.

There comes a time when we have to realize that all we really have is the present. It's the only real place to live. *This* is your moment! *This* is your time to finally make success happen, and see your hard work pay off! Whether you're a brand-new investor or you already have profitable deals under your belt, *this* is your moment to take your business to the next level.

Abundance

Another concept you must understand is that there is plenty for everyone – plenty of money, plenty of connections, plenty of deals, you name it.

You may have heard that real estate investing is saturated, or that the opportunity to make money in this way has passed.

Perhaps you live in a very hot market where investors are a dime a dozen. Let me assure you right now that even if this is true, there is still enough for everyone.

A few years ago I read that if all of the world's wealth was evenly spread out among everyone in the world, there would be enough money to make every single person on the planet a millionaire. If that statement still holds true, then clearly there is more than enough wealth to go around. It's simply up to each person to pursue their share with determination. We *must* dismiss the *scarcity mentality*.

The scarcity mentality says, "I have to get mine, even if it is at the expense of another person." There is ZERO truth to this statement when it comes to real estate investing. There *is* enough property. There *is* enough land.

There *is* enough real estate wealth available for everybody, and that includes YOU!

The scarcity mentality keeps people from ever realizing true success. Having this mentality goes back to what you believe. If you believe that there isn't enough to go around, then you will have trouble seeing all of the opportunities right in front of you.

I've mentored countless real estate investors in the last several years. I can tell you that the scarcity mentality is one of the most dangerous things for an investor to believe. It becomes an excuse for not taking action or not seeing results. Instead of getting creative and resourceful, the scarcity mentality causes people to give up or quit. It also shows up in overly-aggressive fights for deals, even if that means lying or cheating, because the investor believes another deal as good as the one in front of them won't ever come around again!

People will often speak of "opportunities of a lifetime," but let me tell you this truth: these kinds of opportunities actually come around at least once a week. The challenge is not the availability of opportunities, but your ability to perceive them when they present themselves.

Goals

Why are you reading this book at this moment in time? What, specifically, do you hope to gain from the knowledge you will obtain here?

Maybe you're looking to pay off some debt.

Maybe you've been interested in real estate for years, and now you've finally decided to take action.

Maybe you're retired and looking for a new pursuit as you enter the next chapter of your life.

Or maybe you've realized that your job in Corporate America is not actually going to help you realize the "American Dream," and you no longer want to be dependent on a 9-to-5.

Regardless of your motivations, I want to challenge you to get clear on what you want and why you are here.

Sure, most people would like more money. But how will this new income stream from real estate change your life? What will you be able to accomplish because of it? Who will you be able to help and inspire? What mark will you be able to leave on your community?

The deeper you dig, the closer you'll get to the true *Why* that drives you. Don't short-circuit this introspective process, because it's really important.

These big picture targets will help you set clear goals that will allow you to move closer, step by step, to the life you imagine.

I am blessed to have a fulfilling and prosperous career in the real estate industry. At times, the thought of my success is overwhelming, and each day I am filled with tremendous gratitude. I acquired my first property at the age of twenty and in a few years' time I had amassed a portfolio of 17 properties. With those properties, I was generating a substantial passive income while I watched my equity in those properties grow. This would become a part of my legacy.

By that point in my life I had a wonderful, loving, and supportive wife, LaTonja, and we had two amazing children – a son, Immanuel, and a daughter, Imani.

I was on a trajectory for wealth creation that was unstoppable, or so I thought. But man was I wrong! With so much traction in 2005 and 2006, I was not prepared for what was coming in 2007.

A market correction? Inflated values? The market crashed and I watched my portfolio drop from 17 properties to 14. I thought, "Okay, I can recover from this!" But then, my remaining 14 properties dropped to 9.

Again I thought, "This is not good, but at least there is still some positive cash flow. Surely this is recoverable." But the market was still adjusting. Every day the news was filled with stories of financial decline, economic uncertainty, and widespread losses.

The values of my properties continued to dwindle. My tenants could no longer afford their rents. My holdings spiraled downward until my 9 properties became 5, and eventually, those remaining 5 fell away as well, leaving me with only 2 houses.

Do you know what it's like to watch everything you worked so hard for slip away? Have you ever tried to save something that you felt powerless to control? I discovered a bottom in my life that I had not known before. Once the go-to guy for many of my friends and relatives who wanted to jump into the business, I now felt like an utter failure.

I thought, "How could I be so stupid? Surely I could have been more prepared. Why didn't I ask better questions, get better educated, or seek better advice?"

I felt that I had let my family down. This was definitely rock bottom...or so I thought.

However, I was once again overwhelmingly mistaken. You see, while struggling to stay afloat financially, health issues also trespassed into our home. In 2008, not only did I lose my investment portfolio, I also lost my wife. My once healthy and vibrant cheerleader was unexpectedly ripped away from me. I felt robbed. This was most definitely not in the plan. I suddenly found myself hopeless and confused.

I had discovered a new rock bottom.

In this place I had a decision to make. In my pain, I could have acquired a different type of property holdings. There was plenty of land available in disappointment. Places to rest existed in bitterness and despair, but I decided that I never intended to own any property in those territories. So I held Immanuel and Imani and we began the process of healing, growing, and rebuilding. I watched our life come back together one laugh, one smile, and one joyous memory at a time. Our portfolio also grew much larger and faster than the first time around. We were restored.

LaTonja was more than a wife; she was my best friend and business partner as well. In the eleven years we spent together, she made it overwhelming clear that she was always in my corner and wanted to see me succeed beyond my own imagination. Just as important to her was her desire for her children to enjoy a life of love and blessing. From this understanding my passion is fueled. Her legacy is our legacy. Its pursuit is why I build the way I do.

I challenge you to make sure that your *Why* is big enough to keep you here.

So – What is your WHY?

_____
_____
_____
_____
_____

I want to play my part in the process of seeing you reach your goals in spite of personal circumstances that may exist to hinder, derail, or abort your progress. That's really my greatest joy. Real estate is just the vehicle.

This investing game is not hard, and I'm committed to teaching you the principles and strategies you need to be successful. However, even with the right team and the right coach on your side, there will be days when you'll feel worn out or uninspired. That's totally normal! It's precisely at these moments that will you need to refer back to your goals to find the motivation to continue.

When setting your goals, I want you to see beyond your current situation. Challenge yourself to think bigger than you have ever thought before. **Ask yourself, "What can real estate investing do for me that will allow generations after me to continue to give thanks for my existence?"**

If you are focused and diligent, your hard work in real estate will reap benefits beyond what you can imagine right now. Yes, it will take time and a lot of hard work, but if you stick with it, you will make it to the other side stronger and financially independent.

Take some focused time to reflect and write down your goals. Put them here, but also consider putting them in a place where you will see them every day. Remind yourself of these goals consistently to stay motivated on this journey.

GOALS_____

_____
_____
_____
_____
_____
_____
_____

Expectations

Let's take a moment to discuss the expectations you should have for your real estate investing business.

With so many people investing in real estate, it's almost like the "in" thing to do now. Everywhere you turn there are TV shows about flipping houses, house hunting, and renovating. We need to realize that reality TV does not actually give an accurate depiction of reality.

These shows are cut and edited for entertainment, NOT for education.

Often on a reality TV show, you see an acquisition made, a renovation, and then an easy resale all in a matter of thirty minutes to an hour. Trust me, it is not always that clear-cut, and it definitely does not happen that fast!

Another important thing to understand is that fixing-and-flipping is not the only investing method out there, even though that's the one typically shown on TV. Here are a few other investing strategies, some of which we'll explore in detail later in this book:

- Wholesaling
- Buy-and-hold (i.e. being a landlord)
- Lease options
- Subject to financing
- Tax liens and tax deeds

The list goes on and on, but it's crucial to remain focused and disciplined if you want to become a successful investor. This really comes down to following a plan, getting the right guidance, and taking massive action — I'm confident that you can do all three of those things!

My primary goal is to help you find the real estate investing strategy that's right for you.

The first step in the process is for you to answer what I call the "Big Three Questions." Then we'll explore the "Big Three Strategies" so you can see the different ways you can make money in real estate.

Finally, I'll help you evaluate your answers to the Big Three Questions so you can decide which strategy best fits your situation.

You'll also have access to additional resources for each chapter. These resources are designed to deepen your understanding of the material, so we are building on a solid foundation of comprehension as we move through the training.

Ready? Let's get started!

The Big Three Questions for New Investors

Now that we've worked through the process of finding your *Why*, let's explore the Big Three Questions every real estate investor must answer in order to start their business on the right foot.

The three topics we'll dig into are Time, Money, and Credit.

Question #1: How Much Time Do You Have?

Time can be one of the most important assets for new investors, especially if you're starting with minimal cash or credit.

Here are a few questions to consider as you evaluate your personal situation:

- How much free time do you have to invest?
- Will real estate investing be a part-time or full-time endeavor for you?
- How many hours per week or per month can you realistically invest in your real estate business?

As you grow your investing business, you'll need to spend time in several different areas including researching and finding deals, analyzing deals, and growing your network.

Let's look at each of these individually to give you a better idea.

Researching, Finding Deals, and Marketing

First, you'll want to spend some time researching to pinpoint your geographic areas of focus as well as the specific types of properties that you want to pursue.

You'll also be spending a lot of time marketing, both to potential buyers and sellers. As you'll see when we discuss specific investing strategies, it's very valuable to have a robust list of prospects.

Be prepared for marketing to take up a good amount of your budgeted time as this will require you to do things like building rapport with sellers, following up with leads, returning phone calls, and mailing out letters on a consistent basis.

Of course, there are two sides to marketing: *finding the deals* and *selling the deals.* You need to be marketing for both sellers and buyers (or renters) at all times, so that your pipeline stays full.

I make sure all of my students know that marketing is the lifeblood of every successful real estate business. The time you put into marketing is always time well spent!

Analyzing Deals

Once you find a potential property, you'll need to spend time thoroughly analyzing it so you understand how to best approach the situation.

It's very important to consider your "exit strategy" during this phase. This is the way you plan to make money off of the home (i.e. fix-and-flip, rental, wholesale, etc.). Don't worry; I'll explain all of this in more detail in Chapter 3!

Among the things you'll be analyzing on potential properties are:

- The seller's situation and motivation level
- Current value of the home
- Repairs needed (taking your exit strategy into consideration)
- Estimated value of the home after the repairs are completed
- The location (and how easily you'll be able to execute your exit strategy)

Growing Your Network

Finding deals is only the first step! You will, of course, need to bring an end buyer (or renter) to the table to complete the process and collect your profits.

Your success in every aspect of the real estate business depends on the size and strength of your network. **Your network dictates your NET WORTH.** I'll be elaborating more on the power of networking later in the book, but for now, just understand that this is a key driver of your success.

What If You Don't Have Extra Time?

If you're like most people, you don't have a lot of free time on your hands. Because of this, you'll need to focus on **making the time** to pursue your goals, and that will likely involve some sacrifice. But don't let that make you quit! You'll be surprised to see how much progress you can make just by instituting a few small changes in your schedule.

- **Before work (if you have a full-time job).** You could wake up 30 to 60 minutes early each morning, or perhaps work on your real estate business instead of reading the newspaper as part of your morning routine.
- **On your lunch break.** If you have 30 to 60 minutes each day set aside for a lunch break, consider turning it into a working lunch and devoting that time to your real estate business.
- **Limit television.** Take stock of everything you do and ask yourself, "Is this getting me closer to my goals for myself and my family?" If it's not, then put it on the chopping block and replace that activity with something that will move you closer to the future you want.

- **Cut social media or casual socializing (via phone, text, or in person).** This alone can free up hours per day for some people. Even if you don't want to completely disengage from social media, think about setting a time limit on daily engagement so you have more time for real estate.
- **Late in the evening.** Many of my students have families they love spending time with, especially in the evenings. If that's the case for you, it may be a good idea to block off some "you time" to work on your business after your children are in bed.

My Favorite Way to Be More Productive

I highly recommend planning your day in advance to maximize your productivity. If you combine this with the five suggestions above, you will build serious momentum in your business in a matter of weeks.

For me, it's crucial to use this in my own life because I'm always juggling a lot of responsibilities and working toward my "next big thing" as an entrepreneur.

I remember consulting with the owners of a real estate company several years ago. It was a very complex project, and one day, one of the owners commented with amazement that I had all these plates spinning around me, yet I never managed to let any of them drop.

I'll let you in on a secret: *she just wasn't looking when they seemed to drop!*

The truth is that I had to plan in advance what I was going to give my attention to at any given moment. Otherwise, I'd be all over the place, stretched between a million tasks.

My strategy is to focus only on what is in front of me. That's what allows me to perform at my best at all times, because I'm not distracted by past or future events.

As you start doing deals, you'll see that each day is different as a real estate investor. Therefore, it's crucial that you plan ahead, based on your priorities.

Ask, "What is the most important thing I can do to grow my business today?" and then schedule that into your day. During that time, everything else can wait.

Personally, I know that if I don't plan ahead, my day could easily get derailed by one unexpected phone call, and then none of my priorities would get accomplished.

As part of this strategy, I recommend taking time the night before to plan your schedule for the next day. That way, the random events of the following day won't throw you off track.

Before we go any further, write down a strategy you can implement immediately to **make time** *in your schedule for your real estate investing business.*

_____
_____
_____

Question #2: How Much Working Capital Do You Have for Your Business?

Before we dig too deep into the question of money, I want to assure you that you do not need to be flush with cash in order to start your real estate investing career. That being said, having available cash is a tremendous asset that will help jumpstart your business.

Later in this book, I'll share creative ways to get your first deal done using a very minimal amount of money (and still netting a nice profit). Regardless of how much money you have right now, though, it's important to get clear on your financial situation so you can plan for success. So review your finances to determine how much money you can reasonably come up with without putting yourself or your family in an uncomfortable position.

Here are some of the things you'll need cash for:

Marketing Budget

Marketing will fuel your lead generation strategies as you build lists of potential prospects for your business.

Your expenses may include:

- The cost of yellow letters and/or postcards to generate leads

- Postage
- Buying lists of leads from third party services
- Business telephone numbers and voicemail systems

Based on your available funds, decide on a maximum amount to spend each month in this department, and then create a spreadsheet to manage and track those expenses.

Earnest Money Deposits

When you place a property under contract to purchase, you will likely have an earnest money requirement to be paid out of your available cash. This is a deposit you pay that communicates to the seller your level of commitment to follow through on the purchase.

If you close on the deal, that money is credited back to you. However, if you put money on the line and don't close, you may lose your deposit. For this reason, it is important to make sure you're serious before putting down the deposit!

Renovation and Repair Budget (For Fix-and-Flips or Rental Properties)

Bringing a home to current market standards comes with a price tag. In addition, renovations can come with unexpected surprises, like hidden damages to the property. Projecting costs for expected and unexpected repairs will allow you to track your spending and prevent going over budget in your projects.

Carrying Costs (For Fix-and-Flip or Rental Properties Only)

Carrying costs refer to the expenses incurred in the interim period between buying a property and selling or renting it. This is something that new investors often leave out of their equation, which affects the profitability of their deals.

Here are a few types of carrying costs:

- Insurance
- Utilities
- Lawn maintenance
- Interest

For instance, if you can buy a house for $50,000 and repair it for $20,000 and then sell it for $100,000, then you might assume a profit of $30,000. BUT…these numbers don't include the carrying costs that you will also need cash for. These costs add up if you're not paying attention, so it's very important to account for them when you're creating budgets for your deals.

What If You Don't Have Any Extra Money?

If you're saying "I don't have any extra money" or "I don't have enough cash for all of those things you just mentioned," I want you to use the following strategies to keep more of your money so you can invest into your business.

1. **Eating out.** Do you love going out to eat as much as I do? It's amazing how large our food expenses are when we really sit down and think about it. If this is the case for you, consider cutting back on eating out.
2. **Shopping and expensive hobbies.** What about "retail therapy"? Could you free up some cash by shopping a little less?
3. **Other entertainment.** Do you have expensive hobbies? How often do you go to the movies? Do you have any magazine, television, or streaming subscriptions? Unnecessary splurging, even in small amounts, can add up over time and make a significant impact in your financial situation. Keeping a budget can prevent this if you're tracking your spending in order to stay aware of how much money you're spending and what you're spending it on. You can then make the necessary adjustments to eliminate waste.
4. **Selling things you don't need.** You might even consider going through your house or garage, and selling some of the things that you no longer need. If you don't want to have a yard sale, you can go online and find websites or smartphone apps to find buyers in your area. Craigslist and EBay have been around for ages because there is a huge market for this kind of thing! Selling some of your unused goods could provide enough money for upfront startup cash or marketing expenses.

Before moving on to question 3, take a moment to write down some ideas for building up extra cash to utilize in your real estate investing.

_____
_____
_____
_____
_____

Question #3: What Is Your Credit Score?

What is your credit like? Do you know your current credit standing?

The better your credit, the easier it will be to get loans on properties and command low interest rates and great terms. All of these things will help you close more deals and make more money in your real estate business.

That being said, you do not need to have great credit, or any credit at all, to start investing. In a later chapter we'll discuss a strategy I recommend if your credit is less than stellar.

If you don't know your current credit score, you can access it for free via any of the three major credit agencies: Equifax, TransUnion, or Experian. Each of these agencies keeps an account of your credit and payments. They also score you based on how you handle various types of credit extended to you from mortgage companies and credit card companies, as well as for personal loans and lines of credit.

Late payments or defaulted loans can have a negative impact on your score, causing the number to decrease. The more open accounts you have with a history of good standing, the higher the score rises.

Credit is important because it will be required when it is time to finance property.

Financing property can be done with traditional or conventional types of mortgage loans. A traditional loan equally considers the value of the current property as well as the credit-worthiness of the borrower. However, most investors use what is known as an asset-based loan. An asset-based loan is not dependent on your personal income, but rather on the asset itself.

How much income does or can the property produce? What is the value of the property in comparison to what your purchase price and renovation costs will be? These are the most important considerations in an asset-based loan.

Now, even though it is an asset-based loan, oftentimes you, the investor, will be required to personally guarantee that loan. Some asset-based lenders will consider your personal credit score prior to making the loan, so that's where having a good credit score can help you.

Generally speaking, asset-based lenders that require a personal guarantee and a personal credit check are looking for a minimum credit score of 680.

It is also important, from a credit perspective, to understand that there are types of business credit that can be established. However, even as you begin establishing business credit, your personal credit standing will likely also be taken into consideration.

How to Improve Your Credit

The first step to improving your credit is to get your updated credit score and a copy of your credit profile.

You can either go directly to the credit agencies to request copies of your report, or you can use online sites such as Credit Check Total, Credit Karma, or freecreditreport.com. These sites give you access to your report and allow you to monitor your credit over time. They often provide some level of free access as well.

Viewing your credit report is usually free; however, some sites may charge for revealing the score attached to your profile. Just make sure to acquire copies of your credit report, so that you can see where you stand.

Once you get a copy of your credit report, check for any incorrect items you can dispute and get removed from your credit history. This step alone can have a major positive impact on your credit.

Some specific things to watch out for:

- Accounts that were actually paid in full but are still showing as outstanding
- Debt from another person with a similar name as you that shows incorrectly on your report
- Identity theft

Use These Steps to Improve Your Score Month-By-Month:

- Closely watch your credit report to spot any suspicious activity and report it immediately.
- Avoid making late payments. The best practice is to pay your bills by their due dates, but if that's not possible, do everything in your power to keep them from being more than 30 days delinquent.
- Keep your credit card balances at or below 35% of the total limit. So if you have a $10,000 credit limit on a card, it is best not to carry a balance from month to month higher than $3500.

Take some time to assess your credit situation and jot down your discoveries here.

_____
_____
_____
_____
_____
_____

That's the end of the Big Three Questions part of the training!

Now that you have a clear view of your situation, let's move on to looking at the different investing options so you can decide which makes the most sense for you.

3. Active or Passive Investing?

Now that you have thought about your time, money, and credit standing, it's time to pinpoint the smartest investing option for you moving forward.

Remember, there are no right or wrong answers to any of the Big Three Questions.

When you employ the proper investing strategy, you do not need to have a ton of cash, great credit, or loads of free time to invest. Each of those things will help you, but if you're short in one area, just stick with me, and I'll show you how to start doing deals using the resources you already have!

The questions you've answered so far in this book are going to help us determine the best investment strategy for you. More specifically, your answers will allow us to identify whether you are a better fit for *Passive Investing* or *Active Investing*.

These different types of investing require different resources on the part of the investor. If you're short on cash or credit, Active Investing is a great way to start your business. However, if you're short on time but can bring cash and/or credit to the table, Passive Investing may be your best option.

By definition, Passive Investing is "hands-off" and requires little time or effort on your part, while Active Investing requires consistent and ongoing involvement from the investor.

As an active investor, you will likely be making decisions and expending effort every day in your business. For example, as a rehabber you'd be responsible for day-to-day decisions such as:

- Deciding which contractor to hire
- Scheduling contractors
- Property specifics like paint colors, light fixtures, etc.

As an active landlord, your day-to-day tasks would include:

- Screening tenants
- Processing applications
- Collecting deposits and rents
- Responding to leaky toilets or clogged garbage disposals.

Again, Passive Investing requires very little involvement on the part of the investor.

A great example of passive investing is participating in stocks or mutual funds. The investor likely makes some sort of regular contribution, while a fund manager manages the investment and regularly reports on the progress of that investment.

In the world of real estate investing, a passive investor may bring money or good credit to the table while someone else manages the day-to-day activities. In exchange for your money or credit, you receive a return on that investment in the form of some type of interest earned or profit share.

If you do not have the time to actively invest, but you still want to build wealth through real estate, then you are likely a good fit for Passive Investing. The passive investor leverages the time of another person or group of people who play the active role.

Knowing what you do now about the differences between Passive Investing and Active Investing, which type do you think is best for you and why ?

_____
_____
_____
_____
_____

The Power of Leverage

I want you to see your investing career through the prism of *leverage*…

It's okay if you don't have time. You'll just need to leverage *other people's time*!

It's okay if you don't have any extra money at the moment. Your goal is to leverage *other people's money*!

It's also okay if your credit is challenged. You'll just need to leverage *other people's credit*!

The lesson here is that other people's resources can fill in any gaps you have in your own situation.

The Big Three Investing Strategies

"The essence of strategy is choosing what not to do".
- Michael Porter

As I've mentioned already, there are so many different kinds of real estate investing strategies that it can make your head spin. Therefore, it's extremely important (especially for new investors) to choose *just one strategy* and stick with it until they've mastered it.

In this chapter, we're going to review the "Big Three" most fundamental investing strategies so that you can pinpoint the best one for you. Use your answers to the Big Three Questions from earlier in the book as a guide to match up your available resources with the approach that best utilizes those resources.

The first strategy we'll review is Rehabbing/Flipping. This is the process of buying a property, fixing it up, and then reselling it or flipping it for profit.

Strategy #1: Rehabbing / Fix-and-Flips

The rehabbing strategy requires substantial time, money, and credit. If you can bring all of these resources to the table, then this is a great strategy to consider because you'll have the opportunity to make large lump sum profits of $30,000 to $50,000 or more.

The Time You Will Need as a Rehabber

You'll spend a lot of time searching for properties and analyzing possible deals to find one that has high profit potential.

Below are some questions to ask about properties you're investigating:

- What is the area like?
- Is it an active market?
- Are properties in the area selling?
- How long do these properties tend to stay on the market?
- Are renovated properties in this area selling quickly?
- What's the job market like in the area?
- Is the area good for a rental (proximity to grocery stores, schools, expressways)?
- What are the demographics of the area?
- Do the numbers work (i.e., can you buy the property, renovate it, and then sell it for profit based on what other homes have sold for recently)?

Once you acquire a property, you'll spend additional time vetting contractors in order to find those who will do quality work. Before you decide to hire contractors, you'll want to evaluate their:

- Previous and current work
- Ratings and online reviews
- References

After hiring a contractor, you will be responsible for managing them and keeping them on schedule throughout the project.

The average renovation time is three to six months, but ultimately the length of time depends on:

- The scope of the renovation
- The permitting process
- The inspection process in the specific area where the property is located

Then, depending on how you decide to sell the property, you may need to invest more time in the sale process (or you can give a real estate agent a percentage of the sale price to market and show the home for you).

The Cash You Will Need as a Rehabber

You'll need at least a down payment up front in order to acquire a home (if you're getting a loan). Then, once you take control of the property, you'll need to invest money into the renovation.

In my experience the renovation process often costs more than initially expected, so it's crucial to plan for unforeseen expenses. We call these *contingencies*.

Besides the acquisition and renovation costs, you also need to budget for holding costs (also known as carrying costs), which we discussed in chapter 2.

The Credit You Will Need as a Rehabber

Unless your cash is sufficient to cover the entire purchase and renovation cost, credit is also necessary when you are flipping. More often than not, your personal credit standing will determine whether you can borrow money to help with the costs of the project.

Even if you're using asset-based lending (where the lender provides a loan based primarily on the value in the property itself), your creditworthiness will still factor into the decision.

With this info in mind, take a few minutes to consider whether Rehabbing is the right strategy for you given the amount of time, money, and credit you have at your disposal. Write down your thoughts here (get specific).

_____
_____
_____
_____
_____

Alright, let's move on to the next strategy for you to consider…

Strategy #2: Buy-and-Hold

The Buy-and-Hold strategy (also known as "landlording") refers to buying a property and then renting it out to tenants.

As a landlord, you'll primarily need money and credit to run your business.

Why Money and Credit are Necessary as a Buy-and-Hold Investor

After identifying a property to purchase for a rental, you may choose to pay for the asset with cash out of pocket or leverage long-term financing. If you are leveraging long-term financing, you should be prepared to bring at least twenty percent of the purchase price to the closing table as a down payment in order to secure a mortgage loan. This significant down payment is required along with good personal credit because this type of loan is considered a non-owner occupied mortgage, which means that you, the owner, will not live in the property. The thought process is that if you fell on hard times, your priority would be to pay the mortgage on the home you live in as your primary residence before doing so on the property that you don't. Therefore, this loan is a higher risk to the lender and requires good credit and more cash out of pocket.

Additionally, cash is necessary to complete any repairs or upgrades required to get the property in rent-ready condition. Ideally, a good rental investment will only require cosmetic improvements such as paint and carpet and perhaps some minimal kitchen and bath updates. It is important to note that the level of finish detail is different when preparing a property for rent versus preparing a property to resale using the first strategy as a rehabber. When you are flipping a property, it is necessary to finish a home to the standard of comparable flips in the area, complete with all the newest and brightest details. However, when preparing a property for rent, fresh paint and carpet go a long way to encourage a potential tenant to call your place home.

Management

Once you acquire a property and get it rent-ready, time is not a major requirement because this is largely a passive strategy. That being said, there are two options in terms of managing your rental properties, and the one you choose will determine how much time you'll need to invest.

The first option is choosing to manage the property yourself, which involves collecting rents, finding and screening tenants, and making repairs. This could require quite a bit of time.

The other option is to hire a licensed property management company to do the grunt work for you, which will save you a lot of time, but will obviously come with a financial cost.

Hiring a licensed property management company is a great option for a passive investor because, no matter the size or quantity of your properties, they will take care of the things you don't have time for.

Anyone who manages property for someone else must have a real estate license that permits him or her to do so. However, a license is not required if you manage your own property.

The cost of ongoing property management averages 8-10% of the monthly rent amount. In my opinion, this is a very minimal expense for the service that is provided, but you'll need to factor it into your cost analysis when acquiring property.

Cash Flow

Let's talk about *Cash Flow* for a moment because this is the key to the Buy-and-Hold strategy.

Your cash flow is going to be the difference between your property expenses (the largest expense is typically the mortgage payment) and the rent that you are receiving. You also have to consider the various expenses for holding the property, such as insurance, vacancy, property management fees, property taxes, and Home Owners Association fees.

For example, if you're renting the property out for $1,000 a month and your mortgage plus all expenses total $800 a month, then your cash flow is the difference between $1,000 and $800 (cash flow = $200 per month).

$200 a month as a landlord may not be as exciting as a $50,000 payday after flipping a property, but having a consistent passive income stream from rentals is a beautiful thing if you have the money and credit to build up your portfolio. Also keep in mind that the property is likely to keep increasing in value while you own it.

Do you think Buy-and-Hold might be a good strategy for you? Why or why not (be specific)?

_____
_____
_____
_____
_____

Strategy #3: Wholesaling

Wholesaling (also known as "assigning the contract") is a tried and true strategy for new investors for several reasons:

- You do not need a lot of cash.
- Your credit is largely irrelevant.
- You can make quick lump sums of cash (usually $3,000 to $5,000 or more per deal).

However, what you lack in money or credit, you will need to make up for with time and an extra dose of hustle!

Figure 4.1

Behind the Scenes of a Real Estate Wholesale
— an Assignment —

Seller   CONTRACT You the wholesaler

Under Contract for $50,000

You   ASSIGNMENT CONTRACT End Buyer

Assign your right to purchase subject property in exchange for a fee (Ex. $10,000)

End Buyer   PURCHASE Seller

Your end buyer closes on the property directly with the seller at the original contract price of $50,000

END RESULT
→ You make a $10,000 assignment fee
→ Seller gets the full $50,000 purchase price
→ End buyer pays a total of $60,000

How You'll Spend Time as a Wholesaler

A wholesaler finds property to purchase at a discounted price and writes a contract to secure the right to buy that property at the specified price. The wholesaler then finds another buyer for the property at a higher price, and pockets the difference.

For example, let's assume you find a property that's worth $100,000. The owner is extremely motivated for a quick sale, and you negotiate a purchase price of $50,000, which you put into a contract. You then look for an investor who is willing to pay $60,000 for the property because they can still make a profit at that purchase price, even after fixing it up.

As the wholesaler, you would then assign your interest in the property to the investor for $10,000 (i.e. the assignment fee), which is the difference between what the investor will pay and what the seller will sell for.

The great thing about this is that you'd never need to come up with the $50,000 to close on the house and you wouldn't have to apply for a mortgage. Ultimately, you're just selling your contractual right to purchase a property in exchange for a fee.

Wholesaling is what I call "right now money."

Once again, here's how the process plays out:

- Find the potential deal

- Negotiate a fair but discounted purchase price
- Write a contract on it
- Flip that contract for an assignment fee to an end buyer
- Your end buyer follows through on the original contract with the seller

See Figure 4.1.

At this point, you might be wondering how this works out legally.

If the contract has your name on it, how can the investor buy it without changing the name on the contract?

Generally, contracts are assignable, unless they specifically state that they are not. If a seller has agreed to sell their property to you, you can legally transfer your right as the buyer to another person. Essentially, the assignment agreement replaces the old buyer with the new buyer.

Double Closes

Let me guess…you're thinking, "Kito, that all sounds great, but won't the seller be upset if they know I'm making $10,000 on the deal after negotiating them down on their selling price?"

Fair question. The answer is, yes, sometimes the sellers (or buyers) are not willing to complete the deal once they find out how much you stand to profit as a wholesaler. If you're concerned about this, there is a more advanced wholesaling method called a "double close." With a double close, there are still three parties involved. Let's call them Parties A, B, and C.

Party A is the seller.

You are Party B.

And Party C is the ultimate buyer of the property at the higher price (most likely an investor).

In the assignment scenario we looked at, only one contract exists – the contract between Parties A & B. When you assign your interest to Party C, Party C becomes Party B because he or she paid B a fee to acquire their interest in the property.

In a double close scenario, two contracts exist. One contract is between Parties A and B, and it would state (for example) Party B's intention to buy the property for $50,000. The second contract is between Parties B and C, and would state Party C's intention to buy the property from B for $60,000.

You, as Party B, are required to buy the property from A before you can sell it to C. Often these transactions occur simultaneously, or within 30 minutes of each other.

See Figure 4.2.

Why Do a Double Close?

Figure 4.2

Behind the Scenes of a Real Estate Wholesale — a Double Close —

Seller — You the wholesaler

A → B Under Contract for $50,000

You — End Buyer

B → C You find end buyer for property and agree to sell for $60,000

On Closing Day

Seller — You — End Buyer

A → B → C

You buy property for $50,000 and immediately re-sell for $60,000

END RESULT
→ You make $10,000 profit
→ Seller gets the full $50,000 purchase price
→ End buyer pays a total of $60,000
→ End buyer and seller NEVER MEET

The number one reason you'd do a double close is to avoid any confrontation stemming from the profit you'd be netting on a deal. It really varies from deal to deal whether the other parties will have an issue.

I know a wholesaler who went to closing having chosen to simply assign the contract. He was projecting a $12,000 profit with an assignment fee. The seller realized how much this wholesaler was profiting and felt blindsided. She was under the impression the wholesaler was the actual buyer when, instead, he was serving as a middleman (Party B) and making $12,000 on the transaction.

She was so upset that she threatened to not close on the deal. At the last minute, the seller and wholesaler agreed to increase the purchase price of the house, thus reducing the wholesaler's profit by over $5,000.

Take note that laws regarding how a double closing must be conducted vary from state to state. It's also important to note that some states require real estate attorneys to be involved in a real closing while other states allow for title agents to conduct the closing.

Always do your due diligence so you're operating within the legal guidelines of your state for these kinds of transactions.

One last thing – If you were short on cash, where would you get the $50,000 to buy the property before quickly reselling it to your end buyer for $60,000? The short answer is that you'd use some form of other OPM (Other People's Money), which is typically very easy to coordinate in a double close situation.

Does This REALLY Happen, Kito?

Yes! And not only does it happen, but it happens every day for both new and seasoned investors, and it will happen to you *if* you commit to this process!!

As a wholesaler, the number one thing you need is a dedicated amount of time.

Your big time expenditures as a wholesaler will be:

- Finding motivated sellers via marketing and networking
- Building your network of cash buyers and investors
- Evaluating potential deals
- Negotiating with buyers and sellers
- Showing up at closing to GET PAID!

Many people view wholesaling as an entry-level investing strategy. Due to the minimal financial and credit resources required, it is often the place that many investors start. However, in my opinion, wholesaling is also a very appropriate (and lucrative) strategy for advanced real estate investors.

Some people simply enjoy flipping the contract. They aren't interested in buying property and holding it long term. They're not interested in managing contractors, picking paint colors, or waiting for a home to sell on the retail market at full value. They just want to get in and get out with a nice profit.

Plus, what I love about wholesaling is that you learn strategies and techniques you can apply to so many other areas of real estate investing.

As a wholesaler, you'll learn about:

- Renovation and construction budgets
- How to talk to motivated sellers
- How to negotiate with buyers
- How to evaluate properties from a landlord perspective
- What tenants might look for in a property

All of this experience sets you up for long-term success as an investor. For that reason, many people start with wholesaling and eventually begin to venture into other areas of real estate investing.

It's also very possible to scale up your wholesaling business by creating a system that allows you to build a team around you, enabling you to do multiple deals on a regular basis. I know investors who are wholesaling 10 or more properties PER MONTH, so you can see how this can easily become a 6-figure business with a little bit of time and effort.

What are your thoughts about wholesaling knowing what you know now? Do you think this might be a workable strategy for you? Why or why not (get specific)?

_____
_____
_____
_____
_____

Alright, those are the Big Three investing strategies!

I recommend blocking off some additional time to really think about how these strategies fit into your financial plan, as well as your available resources.

# Tax Benefits for Real Estate Investors

In deciding the best real estate approach for you, it's also important to consider the tax implications of various investing strategies.

Reduced Taxes & Tax Breaks

The tax code in the United States strongly incentivizes real estate investing, largely because a stable real estate market is very important to a stable economy. This is a huge opportunity for you as an investor, particularly if you employ the Buy-and-Hold strategy!

NOTE: I am not a tax professional, and the following is not meant to be financial advice. It is important that you consult your tax professional about your personal situation.

The first benefit to the Buy-and-Hold strategy is that the income you receive is not generally taxed as "earned income," and therefore is not subject to Self-Employment tax (or FICA tax), which is the tax that helps fund Social Security and Medicare. **This alone can often cut your taxes by nearly 50%!**

As a landlord, you can also take advantage of what's known as long-term capital gains taxes.

Any time you sell an investment property and make a profit, Uncle Sam is nearby waiting on his cut of your cash. Rehabbers pay more in capital gains taxes because most rehabbers purchase, renovate, and resell inside of a year.

However, when you have owned a property for longer than 12 months prior to reselling it, you can take advantage of what's known as long-term capital gains tax. This is in contrast to the short-term capital gains rate that most flippers pay. **Long-term capital gains taxes are lower than short-term, and you can take full advantage of this tax break when re-selling a rental property after owning it for more than 12 months.**

Depreciation

In addition to reduced taxes in the long-term, landlords can also take advantage of depreciation.

I'm not going to bore you with the nitty-gritty details of depreciation, but you should know that every year you're able to deduct a percentage of a property's value from your taxable income.

Here's how this applies, using the same example that we gave earlier for a property that's renting for $1,000 dollars per month and carrying a monthly expense of $800:

Let's assume that same property has a value of $100,000 and that the land value is about 20%. That $100,000 property has land valued at $20,000 and a structure value of $80,000 sitting on the land. Uncle Sam says that that $80,000 can be depreciated over 27 ½ years, which is that property's economic life.

Here's how that benefit affects your taxes: if you take $80,000 and divide it by 27 ½ years, the result is $2,909. That $2,909 is considered a reduction in the value of the asset with the passage of time based on normal wear and tear. This is called depreciation.

Uncle Sam says that you can write $2,909 off as a depreciation expense each year on your taxes for 27 ½ years. You can deduct maintenance and carrying costs for the property in addition to the depreciation deduction.

Like I said, the tax code is VERY friendly to real estate investors!

If you were receiving $200/month cash flow ($1,000 rent - $800 expenses) from that property over 12 months, then that $2,400 you made that year becomes tax-free because of the depreciation expense of $2,909.

You would only pay taxes on anything exceeding that $2,909 per year. Not only did you get the $2,400 in rent that you can use as cash flow to put in your pocket, you can depreciate $2,909, so you have a remaining balance of $509 in depreciation that you can still use to offset your other personal income to reduce your tax liability.

On your tax return you pay based on your income. If your total income for the year is $40,000, and you have excess depreciation of $509, you will only pay taxes on $39,491.

I cannot overemphasize how big of an impact these tax strategies can have on your short-term and long-term wealth!

1031 Tax-Free Exchange

Another concept, which you can use to your great benefit as an investor, is a 1031 Tax-Free Exchange.

In simple terms, a "1031" allows you to avoid paying capital gains taxes on profits from selling a property IF you use the proceeds from the sale to purchase another property of like-kind.

Here's how it works: You pay $100,000 cash for a property, which appreciates over time. Three years later, you sell that property for $150,000.

Normally, you'd pay long-term capital gains taxes on your $50,000 profit. But when you use a 1031 Exchange, you'd actually use that $150,000 to purchase a new property. Doing this allows you to completely avoid paying taxes on your profits.

This is how many investors play real life monopoly. They buy multiple houses and over time they build value in those properties, later selling multiple houses and rolling the profits into larger structures like apartment or office buildings.

The 1031 Tax-Free Exchange allows investors to continue to push out their tax liability until they are in a lower tax bracket or a more favorable tax position.

Tax-Free Cash Outs

As a Buy-and-Hold investor, you can also take advantage of tax-free cash outs by refinancing a property and pulling cash out of the equity to invest in other real estate opportunities.

This is always easier to understand using examples, so let's use the same example as we did for the 1031 Exchange.

Assume you bought a property for $100,000 (this time you bought it using an $80,000 mortgage with $20,000 down), and in three years it's worth $150,000. Instead of selling the property to get access to your increased value, you may choose to do a cash-out refinance. This means you take a loan against the new value of your asset (the property).

For example, the bank may be willing to let you "cash out" 80% of the equity in the home, which would be $120,000. You'd then pay off the original $80,000 mortgage and pocket the difference.

Even better, you wouldn't have to pay taxes on this money until you sell the home. So you'd be able to take that tax-deferred money and invest it into another income-producing asset.

I hope you're noticing that getting creative is a huge asset as a real estate investor!

Based on what you've learned in this chapter, which of these tax benefits intrigues you the most, and which ones do you want to learn more about?

_____
_____
_____
_____
_____

6 Finding Property

"Opportunities exist all around us; you just have to know where to look." - Kito J. Johnson

Recognizing the profit potential in a deal and understanding how to capitalize on it are two of the most important skills you can develop as an investor.

In this chapter, I'm going to give you an overview of the different ways you can find potential deals to profit from.

On-Market Methods

The most common way for the average person to find property is through on-market methods.

This is when you partner with a real estate agent who searches for properties within your criteria that are listed on the MLS. This approach also includes using platforms like Zillow, Trulia, and Realtor.com to do your own property searches. Additionally, you can tap into the "For Sale By Owner" market to discover more properties, either online or by driving through target neighborhoods and looking for yard signs.

The benefits of On-Market methods are:

- Building relationships with agents and brokerages
- Expanding your network
- Familiarizing yourself with the local market at a deeper level

The drawbacks are:

- Fighting with everyone else for the same deals
- Difficulty negotiating wholesale pricing on properties, due to greater exposure and the sellers obligation to pay a real estate commission
- On-Market sellers typically have higher expectations for sale price, which is why they are testing the market.

Properties on the open market are considered low hanging fruit.

The best deals are NOT on the market. As a matter of fact, when a market is really hot, anything that comes on the market flies off the shelf, and it often sells for much higher than an experienced investor wants to pay anyway.

For this reason, savvy investors utilize off-market approaches to find the best deals.

Off-Market Methods

With off-market methods, your goal is to find a person who wants – or better yet, *needs* – to sell, but who has not yet taken the steps necessary to put the property on the market. A person who *needs to sell* will have some sort of motivational or distressed circumstance.

Absentee Owners

One common off-market approach is to reach out to absentee homeowners (people who own a property but do not live there full-time). You can find a list of these homeowners by searching the local tax assessor's database for owners who have a different tax billing address than the subject property address.

Some people are landlords because they choose to be. Others are landlords because they're forced to be. Perhaps they had to move at a time when the market would not allow for them to sell their property. Maybe their job transferred them, or perhaps they inherited the property. Regardless, this is a great market in which to look for motivated sellers.

Probate

Probate occurs when someone has passed away and there is a court process to allocate the deceased person's assets. In this process, someone is appointed as the executor of the estate by the courts. When real estate is involved, the executor of the estate may choose or be required to sell the property.

Probate proceedings are a matter of public record and can be researched at the local courthouse. Some counties even make these public records available online. Building relationships with probate attorneys can also prove beneficial.

Code Violations

Code violations are notices filed by a city or township against a homeowner who is in violation of some local law. This could be as simple as failure to maintain the lawn, or more complex, like inadequately securing a vacant property for safety purposes.

Local municipalities have field inspectors who ride through neighborhoods sending code violation notices. This, too, is a matter of public record. A homeowner with a code violation may very well be in a distressed situation that would require them to sell their property.

Driving for Dollars

This is another very effective (and simple) way to generate seller leads. You are likely passing great off-market deals every single day as you drive to work or anywhere around town, so be on the lookout for property that may be owned by a motivated seller. Train your eye to do this automatically and you will eventually come across some hidden gems.

Here's what to look out for:

- Vacant or distressed properties
- Unclaimed newspapers outside
- Houses in desperate need of painting
- Broken windows
- Overgrown grass and bushes

When you find a possible deal, write down the address and add it to your "Motivated Seller Leads" list to contact.

Divorce

This information is also publicly available, and oftentimes a divorce ends with the shared property being sold. One smart approach to find these deals is by networking with divorce attorneys.

Bandit Signs

Here is another tried-and-true method to generate seller leads. Bandit signs are the signs that you see on the side of the road that say "We Buy Houses" or "Fast Cash for Your House in Any Condition." These signs are often placed by investors looking for motivated sellers who will sell at a discount.

The rules about bandit signs vary in each area. It's common practice in some areas but illegal in others, so it's very important to verify your local ordinances so you stay in compliance.

Figure 6.1

Off-Market Lead Generation
— for Real Estate Investors —

Method	Contact	New Investor Friendly Score
Absentee Owners	Owner Directly	8
Probate	Probate Attorney	2
Code Violations	Owner Directly	8
Driving for $	Owner Directly	9
Divorce	Divorce Attorney	2
Bandit Signs	N/A Post Signs Locally	10
Evictions	Owner Directly or Property Manager	4

Newbie Friendly Score from 1 to 10, with 1 being the most difficult for new investors and 10 being the easiest for new investors to implement

Evictions

When landlords have tenant issues, they may file eviction proceedings to collect rent and/or force the tenant to vacate. These, too, are a matter of public record. (Are you starting to see a pattern?)

The time between one tenant leaving and another tenant moving in is considered a tenant turnover period. This is one of the best times to approach landlords about selling their property, because their pain will be at its highest!

As a matter of fact, this was exactly the situation when I acquired my first house at 20 years old. I discovered a landlord who had tenant issues. After he filed the eviction, I called him and we negotiated a deal.

Who would have thought that that one phone call would lead to now over 1000 transactions?

In the same way, your investing career will start with that first deal, and that deal can turn into many more over time! There is NO NEED to reinvent the wheel. If you just stick to the approaches I outlined above and adopt a habit of consistency, you will have more leads than you know what to do with.

See Figure 6.1.

Is there anything in this chapter that you didn't know about before? Can you see yourself taking the time to pursue some of these off-market methods? Write down what you're excited about so you can refer to it again later as you move forward on your real estate investment journey!

_____

_____

_____

_____

_____

In the next chapter we are going to discuss best practices for reaching out to these potential sellers in order to convert them into profitable deals.

Connecting With Sellers

Initially you might find it challenging to get a seller to reach out to you. The reality is you are not the only investor trying to convince them to sell their property. There is a strong possibility they have already been contacted by other investors, and have become accustomed to ignoring inquiries.

As an investor and marketer, you must always strive to stand out from the crowd and go the extra mile with potential sellers.

Also, start to notice patterns in what's working and what's not working with your marketing, both in terms of generating leads and building relationships. Take note of the response rates you get from various forms of marketing, as well as from the different markets you're reaching out to. This type of tracking helps you put more energy into the most profitable approaches, and cut the rest.

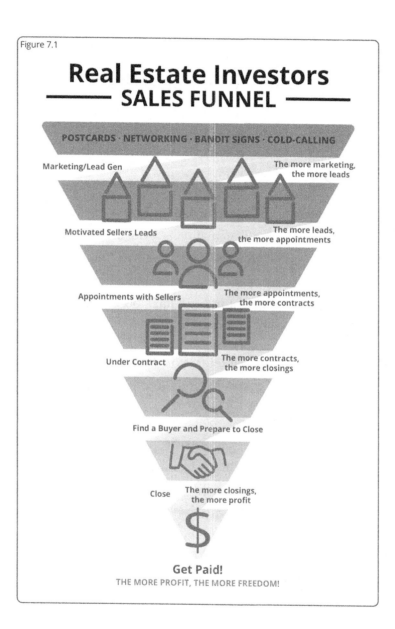

Remember, the only way you can know for sure what will work for you and your market is to get out there and take action! Consistent marketing will yield consistent results.

See Figure 7.1.

Here are some common actions you can take as part of your marketing plan:

Direct Mail

You may use direct mail as a marketing method to reach out to potential sellers (i.e. absentee landlords, landlords with recent evictions, homeowners with code violations, etc.) by sending them letters or postcards.

Once again, testing is key. What works in certain markets won't be effective in others, so try out different wording and different designs to see what sticks.

Your goal is to get the property owner's attention and then compel them to contact you for more information. I've found the best approach with postcards is to be very clear and direct.

You only have a split second to catch someone's attention while they're sorting through their mail, so make sure you stand out!

You may have also heard about "yellow letters." This is a common direct mail strategy for investors. These letters are generally written on yellow legal pad paper. Oftentimes they're handwritten in red ink as well, as this makes letters feel more personal.

Once again, you must capture the reader's attention immediately and tell them the benefit for them if they contact you. You'll need to close your marketing piece with a strong call to action that compels them to pick up the phone (or contact you online).

Make sure to mail your yellow letters in an invitation-size envelope, as this gives them the greatest chance of being opened without being confused with junk mail.

Personally, I've had great success with both yellow letters and postcards. Many other investors in my network have as well. **The key is consistency.** If you want direct mail to work for you, you have to commit to ongoing mailings. This does require a bigger marketing budget, so keep that in mind as you plan your efforts.

Internet Marketing

Social media platforms provide ongoing opportunities to let the public know you are an investor who helps people needing to sell properties quickly.

Depending on the platform, this type of social media message can be shared with your connections as well as the connections of your friends or followers. I have personally closed deals as a result of this type of free social media marketing.

I do, however, recommend that new investors steer clear of paid forms of online marketing like Facebook Ads, Google AdWords, or SEO. Once you get some deals under your belt, you may want to revisit these approaches, but be aware that they often require very large budgets with hit-and-miss results.

Marketing your new real estate business requires focus, and I believe you'll find the greatest success by focusing on the free or cheap strategies we've discussed so far.

Speaking of free (or very cheap) marketing, here's another strategy you should consider using...

Cold Calling

Before talking about cold calling, let me first clarify some general marketing terminology.

When a lead (in this case a seller lead) is aware of who you are and has expressed any level of interest in the product or service you provide, that lead is considered a "warm lead." In instances where the lead has not expressed any level of interest in the product or service, that is a "cold lead."

Direct mail and social media both return warm leads to you. You put out a message, and prospects "raise their hand" with interest when they respond to the message. But you can also reach new leads cost-effectively by utilizing cold-calling and applying it to many of the other strategies I've outlined.

Here is how it works:

- Gather your list of potential homes to purchase or of your referral partners (like divorce attorneys).
- Determine the property owner's name by researching with the local tax assessor's office.
- Search for the owner's telephone number in order to make your cold call.

When I purchased my first investment property years ago, I took these very same steps. The biggest difference then was that I was able to look in a local phone book for the owner's telephone number. Now you will likely utilize some sort of people locator service in order to search for a contact number. This is also referred to as "skip tracing."

A quick Google search for companies that offer these services will yield you many such companies to choose from.

Which of these marketing methods sound doable to you and why? Which ones are you more hesitant about and why? Remember, some of these methods may require you to get a little outside your comfort zone, but the more you do them, the more you figure out what works for you and the more confident you will become!

_____
_____
_____
_____
_____

8 Networking

Your success as a real estate investor will depend in large part on the size and strength of your network.

One of your primary goals in networking is to find a value exchange.

Go back to the Big Three Questions about time, money, and credit. Out of those options, where can you bring the most value?

Let's say you have a lot of time, but very little money or credit (common for new investors). Your goal would then be to network with the purpose of finding someone who will let you leverage their money and/or credit in exchange for your time.

This is a win-win situation for both parties, which is the foundation of all great business relationships.

Joint Venture

In another example, perhaps you have a buyer who's desperate for a certain property that you haven't been able to find. By networking with other investors, you may find someone who has that type of property but who can't find a buyer.

Together you play matchmaker, and you both profit from the deal.

This type of arrangement is called a Joint Venture/JV. When you choose to JV, make sure that your expectations are clear and that you get everything in writing. It's also smart to do your due diligence on any possible partners to make sure they are trustworthy and that each of your business goals complement the other's.

Reverse Bandits

Here is another powerful networking technique to establish your business. In the last chapter we spoke about bandit signs and how to use them to find property. You may also do something I refer to as "Reverse Bandits."

This process would include YOU calling bandit sign numbers that other investors have placed. Let them know you're a local investor, and that you'd like to be placed on their distribution list in case you have a buyer for one of their properties.

The extent of your networking is limited only by your imagination.

However, you need to be careful to approach all networking opportunities with the mindset of GIVING rather than GETTING. You'll build deeper relationships this way, and you'll establish a strong reputation for yourself in the investing community as a result.

Joining a Group

One final networking activity I really believe will help your business is joining a local real estate investment group. Not only can you learn a lot from the leaders of the group, but you'll also be in the loop for available deals. Just make sure that the groups you connect with are supportive and collaborative. You want to be connected to individuals who freely share information and who have an abundance (rather than a scarcity) mentality.

How Do You Find a Local Group of Investors?

Go to Google and look up local Real Estate Investment Associations (also known as REIAs). Most of these groups will let you attend a few meetings for free before deciding whether to join as a paid member.

Go to meetup.com and look for groups related to real estate investing.

Go to eventbrite.com and look for local events related to real estate investing.

As I often say at the real estate meetings and coaching sessions that I lead: **Meetings make you money!**

What does your networking strategy look like right now? How can you expand your network using these strategies?

_____
_____
_____
_____
_____

P.S. If you are in the Atlanta area, I'd like to invite you to join me at my monthly investor training and networking events. We also host and collaborate around the country to create real estate education and networking opportunities. You can get more details on the events page of my website at www.kitojjohnson.com.

9 Avoiding Pitfalls

This chapter is dedicated to helping you avoid some of the most common mistakes new investors make when starting their businesses.

Pay close attention, because this is just as important as the strategies you've learned about so far.

Avoid Unnecessary Expenses

As a new investor, your biggest asset is your time. All the other bells and whistles can be a huge distraction and drain your bank account quickly. So avoid things like:

- Branding and fancy logos
- Expensive business cards
- High-tech website and design
- Expensive marketing that doesn't yield results

Make sure to DEMAND results from the money you spend. If you spend a lot on a website, you should be able to clearly track how much money it brings in. The income from that site should be far greater than the expense of building it.

My advice, especially as you're starting out, is to keep it simple and look for marketing strategies that will cost you time rather than money. Remember, no tool or service can replace your work and consistent effort. So don't let the lack of something prevent you from getting started.

You don't have cash to form an LLC? Get the deal and form the LLC later with your profits from the deal. You don't have money for a voicemail system? Use Google Voice – it's free!

It's not your resources but your resourcefulness that will drive your success!

Avoid Education Overload

Another mistake many people make is running from seminar to seminar or jumping from book to book in an effort to get educated. I call these people "education junkies." Education is essential, but only when you follow up with action!

If new investors learn too many different strategies, it becomes difficult to stick with just one of them. Their minds become scattered. **The best practice is to choose one strategy and master it.**

After you've mastered a strategy (which includes putting systems in place to generate and track consistent income from it), then consider learning and mastering an additional strategy.

Knowledge is power, but only when you apply it. Whatever you do, don't overdose on education to the extent that you never actually do anything.

Inconsistent Networking

Decide right now that you will set aside time on a consistent basis for networking. I've stressed it over and over and over throughout this book, because it really is that important.

Lack of consistency will hinder your ability to succeed. Whether it's real estate investing or any other area of life where you want to see change, consistency determines your results. So get out there and start interacting with fellow investors!

Not only will you have the inside track on more deals, but you'll also connect with possible buyers, private lenders, and people who are looking for partners. Plus, you'll get a great education just listening to other people's successes (and mistakes!).

I can say with confidence that all the money I've ever made in real estate can be directly traced back to my network, and I believe the same will be true for you.

Business, Not Hobby

If you treat your business like a hobby, it will pay you like a hobby (or maybe end up costing you). You really need to approach real estate as a serious business that demands your time and dedication.

The wealth of future generations is tied to your success.

A hobby is something you do when the mood or condition is right. It's something that you pick up and put down when you feel like it, or whenever you have time.

Real business owners don't have the luxury of picking up and putting down different aspects of their business according to their feelings in the moment. Business owners must actively engage in their business on a daily basis no matter what. And that's exactly what I encourage you to do with your new business. Treat it like the massive wealth-producing business it is!

Set Goals

We already talked about this in chapter one, but I also know that many people who are reading this have put off goal-setting until some later time. So I implore you, for your own future success, block off time TODAY to think about your goals.

Get something on paper. Keep it somewhere you can see it. Set a deadline and get to work making it happen!

Here's another space for you to jot down some goals. If you passed up the chance before, don't pass it up now!

_____
_____
_____
_____
_____

10 Your Next Steps

Now that you understand the Big Three investing strategies as well as the value you can personally bring to the table (time, money, and credit), you're ready to choose your path moving forward.

All three of these strategies have the potential to create wealth and financial independence for you and your family. **Which one is best for you where you are at this moment?**

Bruce Lee once said, "The successful warrior is the average man, with laser-like focus".

I've got a mentee who found me after spending over $30,000 on a real estate investor program. In this particular program he was taught more investing strategies than I can count. To this day, every time I speak with him he tells me about something new that he has learned.

I'm sure the education is great, but it's unnecessary and overwhelming, considering where he was at the time as a beginning investor. This same guy, with all the expensive education and all the advanced strategies, was consistently coming to me for clarification and advice. In fact, after spending over $30,000 and finding no traceable success, I helped him through his first deal, netting him a $2,000 profit. Simple focus placed him on a track of success that continues to increase in his now full-time investing career.

So at the risk of repeating myself...

Stay focused on mastering one technique if you want to take the shortest path to success.

Which ONE strategy are you choosing to master first and why?

_____
_____
_____
_____
_____

 # Dream Turned Reality

It's clear that real estate is my passion. I enjoy every day working in this industry. In fact, it's never actually felt like *work* at all.

When I take breaks to relax or refresh, I enjoy traveling to see and experience new cultures. My investing career has given me the freedom to do that. As I travel, I am amazed by how big the world is. There is so much to see and do. My prayer for you is that you discover a new freedom to enjoy life in way that you have not before.

I've been blessed to travel the world, yet still one of my favorite places to visit is Walt Disney World in Orlando, Florida. I've been many times, and I admit without shame that I seem to enjoy it more than my children. I have always been inspired by the story of Walt Disney. It is a powerful and uplifting story of overcoming obstacles, finding motivation beyond the opinions of critics, and ultimate triumph as a result of persistence, commitment, and faith.

Walking the streets of the Magic Kingdom, I am overwhelmed with courage to pursue my own dreams because I realize that I'm standing in the midst of someone's dream-turned-reality. This dream was larger than its founder, Walt Disney, and it thrives beyond his existence as it continues to bring motivation and joy, creating memories for youth and adults around the world.

Several years ago I took a group of young people to Orlando – some of whom had never traveled far beyond their home city – to share in the Disney experience with me. We called it "The Dream Trip." I really do find my greatest joy while fulfilling my role in seeing other people go after their dreams and reach their goals.

There is a ride called "It's a Small World" that I look forward to each time I visit Disney's Magic Kingdom. It's great for a number a reasons. After a hot day of walking the park and standing in lines, this indoor boat ride offers a moment to sit back, rest your feet, and cool down in the air-conditioned exhibit. I also enjoy it because it displays scenes of various cultures around the world complete with the music, language, and style. The ride is rightfully named as it showcases differences around the world while also revealing a common thread in humanity.

The world is a large place, but in reality, it's not so large after all. If you've travelled abroad you've probably come to realize this truth. If you haven't yet, I do hope you will.

In either case, you'll discover this to be true in the business of investing as well.

There are many people in our field. Each day newbies just like you jump into the business, and initially you may feel overwhelmed with the thought of saturation. However, as you stay the course in the business you'll discover that, as investors, we really do serve a small niche in the real estate industry, a niche that is to be appreciated and protected.

I say all of this to make a very important point: I want my students to approach this business as if the marketplace is so large that there is plenty of room for anyone who is willing to believe in himself or herself, yet it's so small that you must make it your goal to work through every deal with the utmost integrity.

The local market in Atlanta is pretty large, but the real estate investing community is really small. I'd also venture to say that this is true in other major markets around the country. The movers and shakers all know one another and are generally happy to network with and support one another. We also talk about our best practices and share our challenges. If we have issues with contractors, tradesmen, or even other investors, we discuss it. And as is true in most situations, the not-so-great news travels the quickest.

My final pieces of advice for you are...

- Conduct business the way you'd like to be treated.

- Don't mix words or over-promise in an effort to secure a deal.
- Don't make promises you can't keep.
- Let your word be your bond.
- Honor those who bring buyers or sellers to you.
- Never try and undercut someone from a deal.
- Respect real estate professionals and pay them what they're worth.
- Seek win-win solutions for all parties involved.

There is always a deal on the other side of the one you are working on. If you treat all parties with respect in the process, it will come back around in abundance. The most successful investing communities are supportive and collaborative, and with that as a focus, we can all accomplish more for the greater good. Here's to your real estate wealth that empowers a dream larger than you in the small world we play in!

Thank you for taking part in this real estate investing journey with me. I look forward to hearing about your future success!

Keep Building!

Glossary

1031 Exchange

A tax strategy used by investors to defer paying taxes on the gains they make when selling a property, providing they use the gains to purchase another property of like-kind.

Absentee Owners

Refers to owners of a property where the subject property is not their primary residence. An easy way to identify absentee owners is by looking for owners whose property tax billing address is different than the subject property address.

Active Investing

Requires an ongoing time commitment on the part of the investor in order to generate revenue for the business. Examples of active investing are fixing-and-flipping as well as wholesaling.

Appreciation

The increase in value of an asset over time.

Assignment Fee

The fee paid to a party contracted to purchase a property in exchange for assigning the purchase rights of the property to a new party.

For example, Party B has a contract to purchase a property from Party A for $100,000. Party B can then assign his/her rights to buy the subject property to Party C in exchange for a $10,000 assignment fee. Party C now takes Party B's contractual position as the buyer of the property.

Asset-Based Loan

A business or mortgage loan secured by collateral or assets, and is less dependent on an individual's personal credit. This is in contrast to an unsecured loan backed only by a personal guarantee (such as an unsecured credit card).

Bandit Signs

Roadside signs used for quick, high-exposure marketing, often attached to telephone poles or stakes in the ground at busy intersections. These are typically the "We Buy Houses" signs.

Buy-And-Hold (Landlording)

The strategy of purchasing property to rent out in an effort to receive monthly passive income while building long-term wealth as the property appreciates over time.

Capital Gains Tax (Long-Term)

If an asset is held for longer than 12 months and sold for a gain, that gain will be taxed at the long-term capital gain rate, which is lower than the ordinary income tax rate (specific rate depends on your income bracket).

Capital Gains Tax (Short-Term)

If an asset is held for 12 months or less and sold for a gain, that gain will be taxed at your ordinary income tax rate.

Carrying Costs

The costs incurred during the period where an investment property is not generating income. This typically occurs when the home is vacant before a renter has been placed (for buy-and-hold) or before the home has been sold (for fix-and-flips).

These costs include (but are not limited to) utilities, property taxes, and interest payments, and they are typically calculated separate from renovation costs.

Cash Flow

The total amount of money moving into and out of a business.

"Positive cash flow" refers to a situation where a business is bringing in more money than they spend in a given period of time. "Negative cash flow" refers to a deficit between the incoming revenue and outgoing expenses.

Contract (Purchase Agreement)

Agreement to purchase real estate for a set price, with set terms (i.e. inspection period, deadline for closing, procedure for repairs prior to closing, financing terms).

Contingencies

The unknown or unexpected expenses to prepare and account for in the budget of a renovation project.

Depreciation

Refers to the diminishing value of an asset over time. In the context of real estate taxes, depreciation is a tax strategy that allows an investor to write off a percentage of the value of a building each year to lower their taxable income.

Earnest Money Deposit

A nominal upfront deposit paid by the buyer upon executing the contract to show commitment to follow through on the deal. Typically, the earnest money deposit is held in escrow and then applied to the buyer's down payment at closing.

Flipping (Fix and Flip)

The strategy of purchasing a property with the intent to add value to it through renovations and selling for a profit.

Holding Costs

See *Carrying Costs*.

Joint Venture (JV)

A process by which you collaborate with another party on a business venture while both parties maintain their independent business identities.

Landlord

The owner of a rental property.

Multiple Listings Service (MLS)

The internal system used by real estate brokers to list properties and share information about properties for sale in a particular market.

While platforms like Zillow and Trulia disseminate information from the MLS, you typically must be a licensed real estate professional to gain direct, independent access to the MLS.

Passive Investing

An investing approach that does not require a time investment on the part of the investor to manage business operations. An example of passive investing is a rental property where an outside property manager has been employed by the owner.

Real Estate Investors Association (REIA)

Local groups of real estate investors who meet regularly to network, learn investing strategies, and share opportunities for deals and/or funding.

Recapture

The system used by the IRS to collect income tax on a gain realized by an investor (via sale of a property) when the investor had previously utilized depreciation on the subject property to offset ordinary income.

Refinancing

The practice of financing an asset you already own in order to capitalize on increased equity, lower interest rates, or better terms. The subject asset may or may not have a mortgage prior to re-financing.

Wholesaling

The strategy of contracting to purchase a property at a discount and securing an end buyer at a higher price in an effort to earn the spread as income.

Working Capital

The financial capital a business has available for day-to-day operations.

Yellow Letters

A type of direct mail marketing popular among real estate investors where an investor writes or prints a message on a yellow ruled paper (legal pad paper or similar) encouraging a homeowner to contact them regarding their home.

Your Six-Figure Strategy

Countless investors have utilized the information in this book to change their lives and the financial future of their families. You are no different than they are. In fact, to have all the foundational information in one resource such as this gives you a significant head start.

At strategic points throughout the book, you have been given a challenge to think and write. Did you? I hope so because if you did, as you were reading, you began the process of creating your six-figure real estate investing strategy.

Repetition and review are key to learning anything new, so below I'm providing you with space to review and gather all of your notes from the book and put them in one place. Perhaps some of your answers have changed along the way, if they have, write your new answers here! If they haven't, repeat your answers from before and refresh your memory about why you wrote those answers. At the very end you will create a summary of your strategy moving forward. Keep these notes and this plan accessible and modify and update it as you learn and grow.

Here's to your real estate investing success!

What do you believe about wealth?

_____
_____
_____
_____
_____

What is your WHY?

_____
_____
_____
_____
_____

What are your goals?

_____
_____
_____
_____
_____

*Write down a strategy you can implement immediately to **make time** in your schedule for your real estate investing business.*

_____
_____
_____
_____

Write down some ideas for building up extra cash to utilize for real estate investing.

_____
_____
_____
_____
_____
_____

Assess your credit situation and jot down your discoveries here.

_____
_____
_____
_____
_____
_____

Knowing what you do now about the differences between Passive Investing and Active Investing, which type do you think is best for you and why?

_____
_____
_____
_____
_____
_____

Considering the amount of time, money, and credit you have at your disposal, is rehabbing the right strategy for you? Write down your thoughts here (get specific).

_____
_____
_____
_____
_____

Do you think Buy-and-Hold might be a good strategy for you? Why or why not (be specific)?

_____
_____
_____
_____
_____

What are your thoughts about wholesaling? Do you think this might be a workable strategy for you? Why or why not (get specific)?

_____
_____
_____
_____
_____

Which tax benefits intrigue you the most and which ones do you want to learn more about?

_____
_____
_____
_____
_____

Can you see yourself taking the time to pursue some off-market methods to find property? Write down what you're excited about so you can refer to it again later as you move forward on your real estate investment journey!

_____
_____
_____
_____
_____

Which marketing methods sound doable to you and why? Which ones are you more hesitant about and why? Remember, some of these methods may require you to get a little outside your comfort zone, but the more you do them, the more you figure out what works for you and the more confident you will become!

_____
_____
_____
_____
_____

What does your networking strategy look like right now? How can you expand your network using the strategies in chapter 8?

_____
_____
_____
_____
_____

Which ONE strategy are you choosing to master first and why?

_____
_____
_____
_____
_____

Summarize your real-estate investment strategy and create an action plan here:

_____
_____
_____
_____
_____
_____
_____
_____
_____

About the Author

Kito J. Johnson is an accomplished real estate broker who specializes in teaching others how to create generational wealth through principles of real estate investing and entrepreneurship. A licensed broker in several states including his Georgia home, his stellar career spans over 20 years and boasts involvement in over 1,000 real estate transactions. As CEO of Atlanta-based brokerage, Buy n Sell, Inc., Kito has been dubbed "the guy to know" in circles ranging from community leaders to elite investors.

Kito was introduced to entrepreneurship at an early age by helping his father, a serial entrepreneur, run his construction business. After high school he started college while simultaneously taking the steps to opening his own construction business. When business took off, he decided to pursue entrepreneurship full-time and withdrew from school. He would later return to college and obtain a degree in Communication Studies from Kennesaw State University.

Real estate was another lifelong interest for Kito, and with his background in construction, it seemed that a career in the industry was always in the cards. He acquired his first home at the age of 20, and from this his passion continued to emerge. Reading Robert Kiyosaki's classic book, *Rich Dad, Poor Dad*, gave him the direction he needed to move forward successfully, and by the age of 30 he owned 17 properties.

He's served as an acquisitions agent and broker for the Blackstone Group's Invitation Homes, one of the largest single family hedge funds in the country, and as part of the 6th largest Keller Williams team in the world. Aside from his impeccable work ethic, Kito's success can be attributed to his unique approach to real estate investing that reflects a healthy balance between risk taking and practicality. He's also a master at networking and developing relationships that encourage the growth of his enterprises.

A brilliant and trustworthy businessman with a heart for people and a passion for teaching, Kito's clients feel confident working with him to help realize their dreams of creating generational wealth through real estate investing. With his signature event, The Generational Wealth Summit, he and his team assemble the best and brightest in the industry for a strategy heavy and highly informative conference about wealth and investing. His goal with the summit and the array of digital courses he offers is to educate and train aspiring investors and the general public alike, on how to understand the market and invest wisely.

The essence of Kito's work is driven by an unrelenting desire to create a legacy of financial wealth and freedom in his community beginning with his own children, Immanuel and Imani. They are his greatest achievements to date, and it is with great pride that he trains them to experience and embrace unprecedented financial destinies. When he's not working tirelessly on expanding his investing empire, Kito enjoys spending time with his family and exploring new cultures through international travel.

For additional wealth building resources from Kito J. Johnson including other books, social media links, blogs, real estate investing tips, courses from the Generational Wealth University, and live events, visit:

www.kitojjohnson.com

Made in the USA
Columbia, SC
18 September 2019